LOVE-IN-IDLENESS:

The Poetry of Roberto Zingarello

LOVE-IN-IDLENESS:
The Poetry of Roberto Zingarello

By

JOHN BRADLEY

SECOND EDITION
Winner of the 1989 Washington Prize

THE WORD WORKS, WASHINGTON, D.C.

ACKNOWLEDGMENTS:

The Anatomy of Water: Contemporary American Prose Poetry
(anthology): "Zingarello Doesn't Live Here Anymore";
Birmingham Poetry Review: "In the Eyes of a Peacock";
The Bloomsbury Review: "Thousands of Shouts Away:
Vallejo in Russia"; *Blue Buildings*: "Window in a Field"
& "Vanity of the Plow"; *Blue Ox Review*: "Patience";
Boston Literary Review: "All for Blanca" & "Epistle to the
Milanese"; *Calapooya Collage*: "In Praise of the Moon";
Calypso: "Why Zingarello Doesn't Fly Anymore" & "So
Many Stars"; *Colorado-North Review*: "Cain and Abel";
Colorado State Review: "Vanity of the Son"; *The Dressing*:
"A Few Things You Should Know about Roberto" & "The
Song of Judas"; *Fine Madness*: "The Kitchen" & "Love-
In-Idleness"; *Germination* (Canada): "Ballad: For Pierre
Magnol"; *Ground Water Review*: "Desire" & "The Sand at
the Bottom of the Heart"; *The MacGuffin*: "On the Origin
of Death"; *March Hares: The Best Poems from Fine Madness,
1982-2002* (anthology): "Love-In-Idleness"; *Mid-American
Review*: "A Few Things You Should Know About Roberto";
Mississippi Mud: "The Curse"; *NRG*: "My Country Is
Not"; *Other Testaments* (anthology): "Cain and Abel";
Poetry Motel: "The Blue Rocking Horse Bar"; *Snake Nation
Review*: "The Wedding"; *The Staten Island Review*: "End
of Days"; *Sub Rosa*: "The Song of Judas"; Talking Leaves
Press Broadside Series: "Ballad: For Pierre Magnol";
Tracks in the Snow (anthology): "Men in Line to Sell Blood,
Apalachicola."

Grateful acknowledgment is extended to Kathleen Tilton
for Tilton House's *All for Blanca: The Selected Poetry of
Roberto Zingarello*, Denver, 1988, where some of these
poems appeared.

I wish to thank the Mary Roberts Rinehart Foundation
for a grant and the National Endowment for the Arts for
a fellowship, which allowed time to work on the original
manuscript.

Thanks to everyone at The Word Works for believing in
this book. And thanks to all those who helped Roberto to
find his way.

For Jana

CONTENTS

"Solitude, my mother, tell me my life again."
—O. V. de Milosz

I

A FEW THINGS
YOU SHOULD KNOW

IN THE EYES OF A PEACOCK

Behind the quiet cage of the sickly peacock,
the shallow light of the ferris wheel
rhythmically sways to the rhythm of a man
worrying his name aloud: *Roberto*, and the light
floods, *Roberto*, and the light ebbs.

In four minutes, Gardenia will leave
the shelter of her ticket booth. Without
bothering to look around, she'll turn,
kick the door shut, pull the hasp over,
slide the padlock down, and click
the stubborn lock home. There, beneath
her left arm, the brown money bag
will bulge, beckoningly.

I take a deep breath, let it go, extending
my hands before me to see them shake.
From the far deltas of the veins that expire
into fingertips, from the feline lengths
of our eyelashes, from the indecipherable
configurations inscribed in our irises,
we stream out of our bodies into the world.

Into the eyes of a peacock, the shape
and form of Zingarello passes. Hush.
In such cases, it is best not to make
a sound. Think only of the empty
ferris wheel seats, rising effortlessly
into the October night, the surprise
in Gardenia's sharp breath.

A FEW THINGS YOU SHOULD KNOW ABOUT ROBERTO

Roberto means, *Hey you!*
And, *Everybody, shut up.*
And, *THIS DOOR IS A PUBLIC EXIT.*
And, Poverty is the smell of the death of six o'clock.
And, In your cranium's darkness, the coconut
white of a cactus flower.

Down the basement, doors lean about
like men in a bread line.
This is where Federico came to hide, in '36.
I rip a page from my pocket Bible,
But Jesus said unto him, Follow me,
And let the dead bury their own dead,
and roll a cigarette with it.
Federico necks with his red guitar
while he plays his "Song While Hiding from Fascists."

> Steer me in the direction of the moon, any color moon.
> Plant in my hand a knife, hard steel, hard wood.
> Who is it, my friend, who is my enemy?
> Tie it to my hand, the knife, so as to gore him.
> Are you, my friend, my enemy?

The basement goes dark.
Some black dog flops down against the basement
window, stealing our light.
Tell me, amigo, Federico asks, like a voice
from a Spanish ballad, *of your beloved.*
Tell me, I reply, *of Andalusia.*

Roberto means, The milkweed down by the pumphouse.
And, *I don't know, comrades.*
I just don't know.
And, sometimes, *Scram.*
Roberto means, My mother slept with a crucifix
beneath her pillow, when she was pregnant,

so her son would be strong.
And, Love is not enough.
Nothing is ever enough.

Roberto means, I'm sick to death
of so much Roberto.
And, I want to be hemlock
so you can, finally, sleep.
But mostly it means, My mother
had one good thing happen to her
during this life, and it had to be
me, it had to be me.

ALL FOR BLANCA

So there I was, Zingarello, the human
time bomb, crouched over inside her
coat closet, nuzzling the soft skin
of her silk kimono. A minor character
in some obscure, minor drama entitled: *All
for Blanca*. The landlady's daughter
gave me the key. *Gas Inspector*,
was all I had to say, flashing my
governmental-green library card.

Everything in the room hushed
when Blanca entered. I could hear
the fleshy rustle of gladioluses,
dripping a bit on the dusty carpet. How
will she ever forgive me? *Just toss
this piece of chalk, striking her
lightly on the cheek*, the psychic
instructed me, fanning herself furiously
with a span of white feathers,
and you'll be free of her, forever.

In the kitchen, Blanca hummed
a simple tune, one a convict might
learn, alone with himself for years.
I remembered that aborigine who sat
in his cell, faithfully composing
The Book of Hope. Using only a needle
and the letter *O*, he worked until
he had inscribed the book into
every square inch of his body.
The guards found him unconscious
emitting a steady, unbearable hum.

MY COUNTRY IS NOT

Blanca, we are not grapes.
Many grapes do not make my country.

The eye of the goat cannot see my country.
Only the swallow knows what the swallow swallowed.

An onion grows in the sea.
The sea, they will say, resembles an onion.

Far away is my country.
Rider with a thousand thousand horses cannot cross it.

In the treetop: treetop, feathers, sky.
Who has not, into his sternum, fallen?

The sun, the moon, they do not darken my country.
The pregnant ones, even they cannot bear it.

Your happiness, Blanca, is another's sorrow.
My country is not a democracy.

The salamander's egg, the egg's careful quiet.
A silence, dear reader, not even you can unravel.

Who has not, in his heart, matchstick?
Who has not, in his stomach, fork and spoon?

My country is not a pasta platter.
My country is not contagious disease.

The eye of the goat is not a country.
Not even the swallow knows what the swallow swallowed.

EPISTLE TO THE MILANESE

On a Saturday afternoon,
I believe, after an espresso
with brandy or two,
the aorta breathes
a liquid restlessness,
causing the dark red
awning outside to flap
so. I believe that
beneath the waiter's
starched shirt, a harsh
desert light bristles.
I believe the moon
was once a lemon,
peeled and left
uneaten. I believe
that high above
the Panama Canal
every year hummingbirds
die from the view.
I believe my mother
when she says she
conceived me in a bar
drinking from
an unclean cup.
I believe J. Robert
Oppenheimer trims his
nostril hairs, just
as I must do. I
believe I've seen
Mr. Ezra Pound, reading
Ovid in a loud, cracked
voice to the bears
at the zoo. I believe
at any moment one
of us could spontaneously
combust—keep away
from saxophones and
dressing rooms where
a dancer calls out:
Honey, is that you?

DIVING FOR PEARLS

Tongues of lettuce
sag, spilling a last
wilted curse upon
our appetites.
Ravaged French
strawberries glow
savagely, parts
of the previous
dishwasher's tired
heart. Wiping my
swollen hands
in a damp dishcloth,
I escape to the open
window, inhaling
the coldness
of interstellar space.
Out in the alley's
close darkness,
a face emerges:
a woman, head
swung back, eyes
shut. Into her
neck, a man's
mouth burrows.
Around me steam
rushes out into
the night, smudging
my scarred shadow
into the brick wall.
Ah, my darling,
sighs the woman
or the man.
Far off, in the dining
room, knives
and forks conspire
to eat the need
to eat.

ON THE ORIGIN OF DEATH

Father Rocco says, *My son,*
you wouldn't happen to know
who borrowed Our Lady
of Beloved Solitude's crown,
would you?

Mother says, *Go out*
to a movie, Roberto. Buy
some popcorn.

Blanca remembers a time
when she was little
and a moth landed on her
outstretched finger.

Mr. Pettrocelli, the butcher,
says, *Zingo. Get a job.*
Then you won't have time
to worry about crap
like that.

Bruno sets me up
on a date with a woman
who has six toes.

Lorca once said death
kisses us on the eyes
while we sleep.

Zingarello says, Friends,
be ready for a sudden
journey—carry
on your person a small
bar of soap.

WHY DOES EVERYTHING HAVE TO BE SO BEAUTIFUL

I never told anyone: *Look into my eyes long enough, and you'll see what's left of the Milky Way.* The honeysuckle never enticed Momo, the milk-eyed boy, in order to drink his muzzy shadow. The crow with a ring around its neck never begs for a sip of grappa. Rilke mails me poems from Duino, lines he needs repaired. On my birthday, fleas spell out across the wall *VIVA ROBERTO* in Gothic, and then leap back to pestilence. My mother washes my feet in holy water and oil, dries them with her hair. Cleo, when I pump the soreness from her silver leg, makes me tango with her in the dark hallway. Should I call you *comrade*, comrade, it could only mean you're entitled to my bread, blood, and morphemic bed—Bruno repaired the injured leg with a tennis racket, so you must sleep on your back like a bored cadaver.

Il Duce's favorite mistress begs me, night after night, to whip her for shaming all Italy. I never said your sister, your shyest sister, is afraid of kite tails. It never once rained sugar-coated almonds after I took my Easter Sunday bath. A wasp never stung me between the eyes when I said: *A sunflower seed has no need of wing or song.* Children make my death mask out of river clay and sell it to me on Palm Sunday. Mario finally married his beloved Darwina, the goat who hummed "The Blue Danube Waltz," and she never let loose again. I never stole *Fontamara* and *Bread and Wine* from the banned book shelf, where they had to display the contamination they protected us from. Van Gogh never stopped by late one afternoon asking for a plum stone and a shotgun shell.

The sound of two women making love in the attic never caused Silvio to go blind. My fear of molting owls was not treated by a Doctor Morpheus, who dines each night on black licorice soup. I never saw my mother toss her wedding ring into the Po. A motorcycle didn't expire when pissed on by a soccer player named Your Weasel. That silverware I stole, I left it all, every piece, in Father Rocco's confessional. *My daughter is not a watermelon,* she told the black shirt, *you don't eat the fruit and throw away the rind.* If I look into your eyes too long, comrade, I see a doll's head with a watch for a brain, *VIVA ROBERTO* on a lichened wall, a cricket repeating what it heard in the rain: *What's wrong with you, Zingarello?* Blanca visits Dino Campana's grave each New Year's Day and recites for him every one of my lines.

THE BLUE ROCKING HORSE BAR

Who killed Zingarello?
they'll ask in that bar in Milan
with the blue rocking horse out front,
the bar where I called for razor,
hot water, basin, towel,
so I could lean
into the bar mirror
and cut myself shaving.
The barmaid would have to
stroke my face
to rub on the bandaid.
Oh, Zingarello, she'd sigh
wiping her hands on her apron.

Who killed Zingarello?
she'll ask the drunk
Carabinieri officer.
Zingarello, he'll shrug,
he can kiss my ass.

But who could have killed him
like that?
she'll ask her glass
of gasoline-colored wine.

Well, I didn't do it,
the drunk insists.
I was upstairs with Rosaria
when they kicked open the door
to tell me. He had to die
just when I was giving it
to her. That bastard
Zingarello.

THE KITCHEN

The kitchen is the most surreal
part of the house. Those who come back
from the dead love the sound of fire
snapping dead twigs, the burning scent
of garlic. That's why I'm here,
my hair so black. It does that
when you leave the grave. I don't know
why I fall in love. Perhaps
it's the wide-sleeved blouse
a woman wears. The red earth
colors in her skirt. Others have tried
to court this solitude. Rilke,
after pricking his finger on a rose,
stood quietly at the sink, watching
his blood softly lap a spoon.

They say the ears and feet grow
after you die. That's not true.
It's just that you can hear purple
rise up the stem of an iris, feel
the many miles the moon keeps
over Alabama. The only thing I know
is the sky and Blanca's eyes
on November 1st are shotgun blue.
The only thing I can assure you
is my heart holds out a snailshell
curling into itself, like the old
woman in the kitchen, knitting
a sweater for her grandson
who died, how many years ago?
The sweater fits him perfectly
if he were alive today.

REVENGE

Oh, Italy,
I need revenge.
Revenge on November 24, 1910,
11:59 PM, the minute
opened, the minute
closed, and I
was born. Revenge
on the kitchen
table in the servant
quarters. Afterwards
they had to burn
the tablecloth.
Revenge on Roberto
Zingarello, the man
who left me, the name
he left me with.
Revenge on Maria Djuna
Lombardo Zingarello, she
who dusted the rooms
in black panties.
Revenge on the cat
under the stairs,
hard as a sack
of cement. For that
they call me Gatto,
he who is afraid
of cats, still.
Revenge on the plastered
brick garden wall
where the Arditi
shamed me. Revenge
on Milan and Trieste
and Rome. Revenge
on you, Italy,
a sink
where they wash down
animal blood.
Revenge on Bach,
and Beethoven, and,

most of all, on
Benito Mussolini.
Though he deserves
something else,
I can't say
what. Revenge
for the whores
with their American
babies they wash
in public fountains
with their laundry.
Revenge on cigarettes
so long and hard and white
and sexless.
Revenge for the sick
with their black
jaguar phlegm.
Revenge on the kidneys,
on their orphan,
orphic softness.
Revenge on the prostate
and all the glands,
their secretions
yellow trucks speeding
through narrowing
streets. Revenge
on the life
too short, the life
too long. Revenge
on the Virgin Mother.
She should have
buried the infant
with her own hands
in the warm manure.
Revenge (no,
I do not forget)
on Katrina,
Greek daughter
of some Greek
professor.
Revenge, too,
on her, but
gently

and not too much.
Revenge for everyone
who had to be born
Italian. They
wanted love and
were fed
lies. Revenge
while we're at it,
on this prison
I live in,
though it doesn't
matter. Nothing
matters.
Oh, Italy,
I love you
like the irregular
heartbeat in the cracks
of the cracked sink.
Like the man committed
for loving
too much. I love you
like the roots
that strangle
my heart, my Italy, my heart.

II

THE SONG OF JUDAS

CAIN AND ABEL

Tonight, to settle the animals
I tell them the story
of the rabbi who renounced
the world, to live
in the company of goats.

I sleep in the barn,
so as not to disturb Abel.
He stays in the farmhouse
day and night, where he studies
the Talmud and the Zohar.

In the morning, I will bring
him freshly boiled milk
in a white enamel cup
chipped on the lip.
Do his books tell him that?

I think Abel studies too hard.
Last night, he yelled:
There's a man in the oven!
I ran into the house.
I saw nothing
but the dark loaf of bread.

Brother, I asked, *wouldn't you
like some tea?*
He stared at me oddly.
*Where did that scar
on your forehead come from?*

I touched the bruise.
*One of the goats
must have kicked me
in my sleep.*

THE SONG OF JUDAS

The laws of the desert
are such: we do not trust
the wakefulness of the owl,
the goat loose in the granary.
Here, let me sharpen your knife.
Have you seen that cockroach
your grandmother carved
from soap? The one who cuts
lilacs enters your beloved
on the riverbank, a towel
wrapped around her wet hair.
All night, Adeema and I
breathed the darkness in
and out through one another.
It hurts, but it only hurts
when I look up, to see
a small thing, a grasshopper,
a dirt road, fleeing us.

To be loved. Not by one.
And not by everyone.
On what does a doorframe
depend? A bit of tortoise
shell fell from the heights
of the cedar. What is it,
friend, you lost, there
in the tall grass? *Judas*,
someone calls, and he wakes,
and I with him. Whatever
the heart is, so is it
not the heart. A needle
clings to a certain stone.
Then, in a moment, lets go.

She was peeling a grape,
pregnant. For some reason
I bent down, and kissed her
belly. Through the cotton
of her blouse, I could feel her
breasts watching me. Passion
has but one cure. The stillness
after passion. A heated blade
laid on a cyst. Here. I
wanted, and I wanted, and
I want.

MEN IN LINE TO SELL BLOOD, APALACHICOLA

You can't sell boredom, or time to kill.
To buy wine, you sell your blood.

Blood is the color of cheap red wine.
Wine makes more blood.

You stand on one foot, then the other.
In the right shoe, there's a pebble.

What do you say on the phone to your mother?
Hello. I'm in Apalachicola.

Who no longer comes, where's he now?
Back to Montgomery, in line to sell blood.

Water fills a man, fills his belly.
But wine is sweeter water.

The walls of the blood bank are hard.
Dawn makes them harder.

It's hard to stand, in any light.
Those alley cats, they have it easy.

They don't have to be men.
They don't wait in line for slaughter.

THOUSANDS OF SHOUTS AWAY:
VALLEJO IN RUSSIA

The steppe, comrades, is black
from the gastric acids
of so many with nothing
to eat. In Lvov,
I bought bread
at the train depot
from an old man with phlegm
in his eye.
He tugged at my shirt cuff,
made me take back my change.
He's right.
What good is money
when someone has spit
in your eye?
Money is sperm
a hanged man throws
away in a fit
of charity,
caritas.

Out over the steppe, stars
are Russian villages
I will never get to,
thousands of shouts away.
That pale fish,
once my face in the window,
glides over the filth
on the sea floor.
It's not my fault, I yell
through the conductor's larynx.
It's not anybody's fault.
Another baby's cry.
I can hear it, all the way
from Peru.

THE ECONOMY OF LOVE:
LETTER TO EZRA POUND

One grape, Ezra,
is worth how many heartbeats of earth?

A man, say,
for one season, a decade, his lifetime,
picks grapes.
One canto, then,
equals how many bushels of grapes?
The Collected Cantos, then, equal so many
laborers, divided by so many liters
of bread and wine, subtracted
from the cost of lightning, over the cost
of rain, multiplied by the songs
of so many crickets per hour
per square foot?

Mussolini's footprint, you say, was so big
Gandhi could curl up inside it, and still
have room for his Bhagavad-Gita, his loom,
and, one on each side, his granddaughters,
to keep him warm.

The woman, Ezra, who sweeps the cathedral
in Taxco, what does she leave
the warm sleep of her husband for?
And the silver in the mine beneath
the cathedral's marble floors,
is it true the priests sift
the soft mineral into the flour
of the communion wafer?

Those streetsweepers, who speak
with their brooms to the streets
of Vera Cruz, discussing the weight
of a hummingbird feather, the prophecies

of a certain Norwegian pine,
the etymology of the word *manna*,
the desert bread, how it traces back
to *hand*, what is it these men pour
into their midnight coffee?

In the corridors of St. Elizabeth's, Ezra, you
smell of cabbage, boiled by Jews in Polish ghettoes,
of cattlecars where Jews in Rome fouled themselves,
the sweat of blacks down in the basement
of the Philadelphia mint, who melt their labor
into bricks, into blocks of gold.

Whatever it is that money cannot possess,
the bare feet of the magnolia's husky breath,
the black coffin afloat in the eyes of a goat,
where Isis gives birth to the black eggs
of mountains, the miles of intestinal thought
in the head of a red cabbage, the nighthawk's
cry caught in the throat of a mandolin,
that's what I want, Ezra, nothing else.

Can money ever
roar the lemon's yellow?

Place your arm, lightly, around the shoulder
of the gardener, as you strut the hospital
grounds. The impatiens, patiently impatient,
wait for you, and no one else, Ezra, to touch
them open.

WINE IN THE CUPBOARD

So that's how Cleopatra
grew in beauty. Other
women rubbed into her

jealous legs their
honey. The universe
must revolve around

something. The pitcher
of wine stored below
the sink. You come in,

friend, late and panting.
It's there. Jesus
hid his love inside

the flea. My father
once shot a cat.
That's why my kidneys

are a loan, the weight
a desire brings.
Another desire: the red-

haired woman glimpsed
in the woods of my red
geranium. Page by page,

a man searches
through this book.
Zingarello, he calls

into the pitcher's tilt.
But who will go down
into the long, dry roots

of the wine, far below
the earth's thick sleep?
You? Me? The question

leaks from its tip
an oil, not solely mine
but a psalm the body makes
ours awhile.

VANITY OF THE SON

"Please die, mother, so I may love you more."
—Rocco Scotellaro

I know the scent of my mother's flesh,
    the vial of holy water beside her bed.
I know not to look, when she bends to scrub
    the kitchen tiles, but I know I will,
    to see the black moon rise over the fields
    there, between her breasts.
I know the long loaf of bread floating up the stairs
    in the hand of the drunk, who stumbles
    into her bed.
I know the woman who slept with her husband's bull
    so that a calf could be born in the spring.
I know Lake Superior, how it narrows into Duluth harbor,
    swims up the St. Louis River, where countrymen
    bleed the brown blood of the paper mill.
I know the blind dive of swallows into drainage pipes
    to burst out the other end, through
    that thin slice of sun.
I know the taste of fresh milk, scooped from the white
    thighs of that girl who sat across from me
    in French class, her legs slightly parted.
I know how to lie like the centuries
    at the bottom of the Dead Sea, so my enemies
    cannot find me.
I know about aborigines, how their stunted tails wag
    at the scent of water three days distant.
I know about the babies of the nuns, hidden inside
    the desks of schoolgirls accused of giving birth
    in class at the sight of a scrap of the Shroud of Turin.
I know how to make a girl sick for me, stroking
    with a stick the crook of a sycamore,
    saying her name aloud, knowing all the time
    I'll regret this.
I know the dry stickiness of Mediterranean nights
    in my mother's shaved armpits, the scent
    of a Greek slave who dances in the tent
    of a Roman general.

I know how fruitflies cling to her groin
        to hide her sex from the eyes of gods
        and godless men.
I know how she rises, to braid her hair each morning
        so the sun can climb out of its darkness.

* * *

I know the need to migrate to America,
        to sit on a rotting wooden porch
        in Pascagoula, sucking on a Lucky.
I know the secret of salmon, to run
        getting smaller and younger as they approach
        the place from which they shall go forth
        into this world once again.
I know about bear sperm, how it moves
        downstream, up the legs of bathing women
        to impregnate them with wild, hairy
        children, who run off to live
        alone in the woods.
I know the boys who crept into the church vault
        during their funeral, to eat the hosts,
        washing them down with communion wine.
I know the basement bar where the dead
        babies of the nuns smoke cigars
        and throw dice for beers.
I know the ladder that climbs to the hole
        in the sky, where everything
        that ever happened, or will happen,
        is written down in *The Book of Days*,
        left open on a table set with bread,
        honey, and dagger.
I know every grain of sand in *The Book of the Gobi*.
I know every man Blanca ever slept with,
        how many scars it takes to make a heart.
I know the smell of those men in black
        who find comfort in the smell of other
        men in black shirts.
I know the boy who hid himself in birdseed
        his mother tosses to the winter
        birds, that he might see the dawn
        from every tree.

I know my mother's name, Maria, means *bitter*.
　　But I will never tell her.
I know the sin worse than murder, to want
　　to sleep inside the woman
　　who gave you birth.
I know, when I die, her hands shall cover
　　my eyes with black soil.
I know the length of infinity.
I know whosoever holds a drop of light
　　swallows the seed of the father.
I know the desert to come.

THE WEDDING

Don't do it, Roberto.
I lie back on her bed, the quilt
white as a bride's, and I listen
to her slowly become beautiful
as she puts on her makeup.
Whatever you do, don't
get married. She pouts
into the mirror, lipstick
wet on her lips.

One kiss, and you think, this
is it, I'm in love. Another
kiss, and you're married.
One more kiss, and there's
a baby in the bed, howling
like the souls in eternal
torment. God bless them.
Roberto, don't do it.

Your father and I, we
got married in a hurry.
We dined on pasta with anchovies,
then dashed to the chapel.
We had to wake the priest.
Your father so serious
in his uniform, me in my black
evening gown. Sure, I'd do it
all over again. Those first
years, they were charmed.
But marriage? I'd be better
off now if I sold it.

How do I look? Zip me
up in the back, honey. There's
some chicken in the icebox.
Lord, your hands are cold.
Don't tease the poor cat. Take
a bath, but don't use all

the hot water. The neighbors
complain. Come, give me
a kiss. Ciao. The girls
are waiting.

FRAGMENT: FOUND WRITTEN INSIDE ZINGARELLO'S *THE WIT AND WISDOM OF IL DUCE*

My head is a sheet of glass
behind which you can see the infinite
undertow of frenzied ants.

My head is a field of asparagus
where a parachutist sits, unable
to rise for fear of falling
back from where he fell.

My feet perpetually circle the city
block where handouts of coffee and day
old rolls emerge from an opening
in an unmarked wall.

My feet lie dormant inside a box
in the Milan Post Office, on a shelf
with other boxes, stamped in red:
ADDRESS UNKNOWN.

My heart is an eggplant, wrapped
tightly in a black shawl, pressing
into the belly of a woman
I do not know on a crowded bus.

My heart is a bathtub filled
with red wine, slowly digesting
a sheet of music by Satie
singed by a feral heat.

My sex is a letter, the last
written by Mussolini
to his coy mistress: *My Dearest
Clara, if only you were a pheasant,
and I cradling my shotgun.*

My sex is a telephone, endlessly
ringing in the African bush.
A lion glares disdainfully
upon such a puny, fearful bird
that can't even lift itself
back into the boundless sky.

WHY ZINGARELLO DOESN'T FLY ANYMORE

Seriously, I prefer to walk. That's right. If it's tales of soaring through the atmosphere you want, well, don't come to me. I'm just not interested. What interests me? How to swim, naked and human, beneath this black earth.

I used to fly, they tell me. Some blame it on my blood, a gypsy relative on my mother's side. A long nose and crooked teeth, that's all I can remember of her. Others say I hallucinated—hallucinated the class into hallucinating the sight of me flying. My teacher, she said I did it to get attention. The doctor rubbed me on the head and said it was nerves, aggravated by poor diet. More greens, he advised. My mother, she just shrugged, and quietly said, *Roberto, stop eating dead birds.*

Geography class, those pictures of the Nile, pyramids, pharaohs. The smell of eucalyptus cough drops. And that word: paper made as thin as the skin of those mummies, that word: *papyrus.* I was rolling around on the floor, kicking desks over, drooling, the kids said. Then I was up near the ceiling, my blue silk scarf trailing behind me. Sister ran and came back with Monsignor. He led the class in an *Ave Maria*, my favorite hymn. I floated back down to my desk. The class applauded. Monsignor said it was a miracle. Then he sent me home.

It's so much easier to walk. Nobody notices you. You might have hidden on the tip of your tongue a wedge of lime. Right there, inside your shirt pocket, you might have the number 5, pried off the front of the downtown police station. You might carry a mouthful of salt water, ready to leap into the face of the next Italian who dares breathe garlic at you. As long as you keep your feet on the ground, you can get away with anything. But, if you fly, some bastard is always waiting to shoot you down.

I used to fly, they say, about three feet off the ground, along railroad tracks, usually, on the lookout for buttons, coins, a ring. A ball of tinfoil that passed through the belly of a crow. The purple ribbon that slipped through the long hair of a woman in a breeze. That sort of thing.

All in all, I'd rather walk. Curl my arm around a lamppost, rest my head on the shoulder of a prostitute, press my brow into the damp moss beneath a bridge. I'd rather smell the fragrance of the urinal in the bar, my comrades' scent, the same as my own. Feel the earth reel beneath my feet, and know, if I fall, she will embrace me.

Flying isn't all they play it up to be. First, it leaves you irritable. The door blows shut, and you want to slap somebody's head off. Secondly, it depletes the iron content in your blood. The flying gets higher and higher, the body weaker and weaker. Thirdly, it creates a false sense of euphoria. Even Italy looks beautiful up there.

That's why I can't sleep at night, unless I take two shots of blackberry brandy, grandfather's remedy. To close my eyes with my hand clutching the leg of the kitchen table, and know—even then—the kitchen table and I might both be flying! Blackberry brandy eases you down, increases the pull of the earth on your body.

If you've got to know about flying, go see Bruno, the orphan. Why, he can leap off the watertower, and land unhurt. Or, at the zoo, study those ungainly birds with their heads thrust down, under this earth. Or, better yet, speak with Blanca. She can tell you all about flying. Me, I walk.

III

IT'S ALMOST FOUR O'CLOCK

PATIENCE

Have you ever, within your body,
ever been naked, like water,
in your stomach, in the shape
of a horse? And is the body ever
within your body, totally alone?

Whatever, then, has content,
has form, also grows tired.
Tired, not once, but thoroughly
like the black hair found
in the empty shoe. Like the voice
a woman left in the corner
of the closed shoe repair shop.

Even what is most exhausted
is tired, not patient, but
a kind of patience. Have you
ever, once, with your lips,
kissed, with nothing but
patience, your own stomach?

My sex, I let it go, once,
to bring back what I cannot
into my body. It's there
at the door, holding out
a tree limb. *Thanks*,
I say, *but I'm not hungry*.
It gnaws on the wood. Thus
a tree enters my stomach.

You, who are soft,
rubbery as exhaustion. Look,
as you float, black, inside
and out. For whatever flows
into the stomach goes black,
like fingerprints on a grape.
And what goes black cools,
back into the street's sky.

I am greasy and wavy
and old, the soaked bean,
misshapen and enlarged
from your exhaustion.
Behind your back, behind
your stomach's back,
I am the face made
from boiling the bag
your stomach is, in a bag.
Like a stickiness on
your shoe sole, I cannot
leave my wanting of you.

Like a nun, unraveling
her blood, strand by strand,
wherever I am, again
and again, is yours.

FROM A RED GERANIUM NAMED ISABELLA

Because red, Roberto, even my red is not big enough to contain all the books of psalms stored within you. When my red spreads over your lips, the sofa gives. In Milan, Prague, Cleveland. The eggcup, on its shelf behind the stove, leaks a desert longing. The hairs on your mother's wig darken. And into his bowl of chicken noodle soup, the mortician frees a tapeworm.

The only path to loving a plant, Roberto, is to live for a while as a plant. In the stillness of the cathedral, death smells of the blossoms it has grown. And so the flowers and their coffin must be burned together. Beneath the hush of the poplar, you scattered from a paper cup the ashes of the boy who slapped his own grandmother. That boy waits for you there, still.

It does no good to think about it. Go out, and go down, into the basement. Sit, and read, with your fingertips, the moss spreading over the ribs of Rilke. Listen to what the walls say about you: *His mother was a paramecium. He speaks spinach in his sleep. He never once made love to the morning glories! What do you expect from a walking root?* Humility means you have not, Roberto, gone far enough down, into the earth. Go deeper, child, deep.

You cannot love another until you have known the face of the table, feel the jar of cold grape jelly, the young son rubbing his delicate groin, the anger in his cup of coffee, driving him away from the calm hum in the table's wood, the curved embrace of the spoon.

You cannot fully love until you know the belly, the deep swirl of the blood and its restless pacing. To be filled with nothing but the deep, intimate *you.* How we long to be something else, anything. To hold upon the tongue: *trowel, tangerine, accordion.* And make the joyful claim of the hammer: to be of use.

Roberto, someone calls. You stop, turn. No one. Not the tiniest sand flea, from which all things were born. Then, out of shadow, a girl, daughter of a doorway and a plum. *Chiclets?* she says, and you kiss her, on the top of her head, saying, *Isabella, my Isabella.*

IT'S ALMOST FOUR O'CLOCK

And I'm busy, as usual,
holding my glass of wine
red, like the hour. I watch
thirty-four years turn
toward thirty-five, an age
when it's not necessary
to wear socks.
The waitress's thin
fingerskin cracks, proof
she has spent too much
of her hand's life
in the sink, dry
and lifeless as the fire
in a firefly. If she
was born in an olive
grove, tonight
I'll marry her, here
on this table, round
and grainy like vodka.
What's important
is the unimportant
little thing. How
does the scallion know
it's not a scallion?
Why does the road,
sometimes, when no one's near,
cough quietly to itself?
And that long black
skirt draped over
a cypress on
Van Gogh's Way.
That cypress where
the Virgin stepped out
to press her cool
hand to my forehead,
asking, *Are you*
all right, Roberto?
My face full,

like the moon's girth.
Like the internal
emptiness of a pump. Proof,
as is everything,
of something.

SO MANY STARS

Rhonda, Spain, January 14, 1913

    In winter, Katharina, the heart
contracts. The night expands.
Ronda *is* round, a column thrust
thousands of feet above the dark
plains below. Last night, on
the edge of the plateau, I heard
one of the unborn, calling out
from an ungathered potato
to a roaming farm dog: *Leave
me alone.*

        I closed my eyes. So many
stars, so many ways to die.
The night poured into me
from all sides. My flesh went
dark and cold. I was no longer
Rainer Maria Rilke, but pine
cone, alula, iron ore.
I was most a blind needle
on the leaf of an aloe.

           Katharina,
what are those frozen sutures
seared in the skull? What
do they foretell? Though
I had the chance, I stumbled
back, away from the cliff's
edge, and breathed out stars.

IN PRAISE OF THE MOON

The moon
must be served
alive
in a basket
covered with hot
white linen.

The moon
must be broken
into pieces
stabbed
with the teeth.

The moon
must be eaten
slowly
so it won't
kill you
all at once.

HOW I BROKE VAN GOGH

It was easy. He
was a sincere, simple
man. I felt a sympathy
for him, for the earth
he carried inside
his shoes. He only
wanted what God
could not give.
The cornfields,
the veering crows,
the shimmering light
of the coming storm,
the breathless wind.
But none of this broke
Van Gogh, none of this
drove him. His skin
smelled of onions
and sweat. On his neck,
a red welt. *Vincent*,
I called into his brain's
soft folds. *Is this*
what you came here for?
This is your birthright,
Vincent? The cornstalks
shivered. Vincent
lifted one shoe, cut
a scar into the damp
soil. I kissed his
cheek, I held his arm
for a moment, then
turned. The gun blast
stumbled against my
coat, pushing me
away.

THE CURSE

A curse upon you, Roberto Zingarello! she flings down at me, from her fire escape. It swirls along my spine, cold, like the cup of coffee, the color of her dirty laundry water, her husband chokes on in the morning, but won't let her take back. With the toss of a flowerpot, she seals my curse. If I wasn't damned already, I am now. To have a red geranium die for your sins. *May your God and your Devil mate*, I mutter, *giving birth to a Great Stillness.*

Like the ice-pick-blue Jaguar, smelling of the fearful lust of the kid who violates and then abandons her to an alley, I ponder the curse, not only mine, but upon us all since before the first Darkness. From a glass on an empty café table, I lift an ice cube, *Hereby declaring you the property of the people of all Italy*, and swirl it on my tongue. The curse, why it's nothing more than a fishhook frozen inside this cube of ice my body's heat slowly dissolves. What is fame? The refuse of a meal picked over by one of those erotically starved, known as, what else, Zingarellos.

Ah, Fortuna. I hand over the piece of fish I pocketed back at the café to the calico, following me like my fate. To fall in love with love, only to die, at the end, alone, hugging the damp sheets. I want my assassin to declare in public his infatuation with me. I want to fall on my knees in the street, swallowing the pain, for once, so it may pass. And I want, finally, for Blanca to hold me, the way Felice did that time on the railroad trestle.

And just who is this Blanca? The calico flees at her name. Every woman I have ever loved. The red ten speed Bruno ripped off, but couldn't give away. Every woman I have ever loved who can't love me. Whoever she is, it's for Blanca I get up in the morning, for Blanca I stand in the window, and deliver my blessing unto the world, in the voice of Kabir: *You bastards, I know you're out there.*

Because, comrades, they are. And I don't just mean those six bullets that took Lorca, buzzing now the blossoms of the almond tree, waiting to silence my blood's babble. A block of ice slides over the dry throat of the street. What is love, but a malediction. The hollyhocks, who bloom, without ever being asked, from every side. What you give, when you have nothing more to give. The scent of lemon cake in a courtyard draws me. I have this terrible fear of coming back, after I die, as Zingarello.

LOVE-IN-IDLENESS

In the rusted railroad
shack, Bruno loudly
introduces each
cockroach racing
tonight.

       I listen
carefully, taking that
misshapen cinder, that
twitching finger
as a sign.

      Biting
down into another
sugar cube, I watch
my cockroach, Love-
In-Idleness, come in.
My shadow sways.

      *

Six eggs surrenders
the tobacco-stained hand
of the eggman
into mine.

       The yolks
tremble at the hunger
murmuring in my touch.

After we die, the ancient
Egyptians say the heart
shall be weighed
against a feather. How
thin this eggshell
beneath my fingernail.

ALONE WITH MY INTESTINES

What is it down there
my intestines try to tell me?
I don't want to know
who Blanca is sleeping with tonight.
The only thing that keeps
the Great Wall from collapsing
into the Sea of Tranquility
is the color after white.
Two plus two never equals
only four. Look into the left
eye of Jesus, and you will see
Judas, before he learned how to
seduce you. Roberto, the only thing
that keeps you from the lips
of Rilke is Roberto. Rilke knew
more about love than all the laws
of Einstein. No one can
tolerate the proximity
of his own intestines
without first glancing over
at the yellow canary, perched
on his right shoulder.
Last night, I found a saxophone
stuffed with dirt.
Does this mean I'll die
with a tiny wet spot
on my fly? The only thing
that keeps me from crawling into the *o*
at the end of *Roberto*, that keeps me
here with you is that
I love everyone so much
I really don't give a shit.
Like the nightwatchman
stroking the worn brass key
to the unmarked door.

THE SAND AT THE BOTTOM
OF THE HEART

And he knew, he was very near the sand
which meant—he was very far from the bottom.

And he knew, he was very far from the sand
which meant—he was very close to the bottom.

He could see
particles of sand, larger
and smaller than red
grapes, every pore
in every particle
swelling out, then
swelling in, sand
sifting through
the opening
and closing of each
opening.

And the heart was trying to fill out a job quality control
report, but the heart couldn't get past the first question, the
heart didn't know if it was European or Hispanic or Asian
or African or Other, the heart didn't know whether to
check *M* or *F* or both or neither, and the heart didn't know
who to consult.

And each of the sand particles
busily flowing in and out
of the pores of sand appeared
to be thinking: I, too, am part
of the heart, which meant—
they were not thinking at all.

And the part of the heart which needed to love
was very sad, which meant—it was quite happy.
And that part of the heart which needed no love
which needed nothing but the working of the heart
was quite happy, which meant—it was very sad.

And the heart knew it was very near the bottom
which meant—it was very far from the sand.

And the heart knew it was very far from the bottom
which meant—it was close, so very close to the sand.

IV

ZINGARELLO
DOESN'T LIVE HERE ANYMORE

THE DIMENSIONS OF THE HEART

I want to measure out the blood
in my heart
into a row
of shotglasses.

I want to translate its weight
into grams of rice,
into the number of days
I could live
on those rice grains.

I want to convert
its thirty-eight years'
heartbeats
into wingbeats,
into minutes the hummingbird
might loiter in the mimosa.

I want to calculate exactly
how many beats
my heart has left
and then count them off
one by one.

BALLAD: FOR PIERRE MAGNOL

When I die
bury me
in the magnolia,
in the waxy leaf
of the magnolia.

Don't listen to me.
Listen to the rain
wear at the earth.

Listen to the earth
slowly breathe.
Don't listen to me.

When I die
bury me
in the fire ant
on the wet magnolia.

ELEGY ON THE DEATH OF A MAD DOG

Shoot me,
you said, Benito, to the partisans,
shoot me in the chest.
In the descending aorta,
the thigh, collarbone,
neck, thyroid, and right
arm. Nine shots in all.
Why? For the crime.
You wanted it all. All
or nothing. Nothing
at all.

In the cold
waters of Lake Mera,
the fisherman found them,
your rings. The wedding
bands of your Italian
brides. Remember them?
You had to marry them
all. *Tutto, tutto.*
You had to seduce them
all. You and me,
Benito. All or nothing.
Nothing at all.

Now you hang
in shame by your feet,
from a girder, a bombed
gas station.
The crime: not enough
love. The accusers:
Rachel, Edda, Claretta.
Wife, daughter, whore.
All and nothing.
Nothing at all.

They dumped
you from a yellow van
into the square.
The bastards you sired

on every street.
The ones you tried
to flee. (You, of all
people, Benito, should
have known. Never
turn your back
on a bastard.)
The crime: Sunday,
29 April 1945. Milan.
Piazzale Loreto. All
for nothing. Nothing
at all.

Now the same
women who once lifted
their skirts for you,
Benito, beneath bridges,
stairs, immense posters
of you, do so one last
time, today, as they
squat over your face,
Il Duce. To leave
their scent. The stink
no one can resist.
For the crime is always
the same. Never
enough. Me too, Benito.
All the love, or
nothing. *Me ne frego.*
Take it all.

WINDOW IN A FIELD

From the bed under the glass
window in the field, you can see
exactly what you are not:
the muscle sewn into the bone
so the goat cannot get away.

There is no other way
of measurement. The stars
stain the back of the retina.
Berries of burnt blood taste
of winter stars. I have no
right to ask. But whose
animal skin now covers
at night the burning legs
of my sister? Friend, you
do not answer.

I know. Always the ones bent
over the chopping, raw
soreness of field. And that
other one, sleeper who wakes
here, peers out his window,
and falls back, upon his pineboard
bed, fainter and fainter.

Against these earthen walls,
rows: onions, peppers, dawn-
smudged turnips. Who lives here
more than woodsmoke twistings
for fingers. Fire
his only motion. No one
lives here for another.

Muddy feet, reddened
knuckles, shirt-load of turnips, go.
Go home. Which is not here.
What is here recedes, settles,
congeals in the indentation

of an ox hoof. What is left:
an arm, overlarge, overweary,
floats across the back
of someone's sister, perhaps
once mine, once yours.

VANITY OF THE PLOW

Whether it's true or not,
it's true. They cannot be given up,
those stains on the blade of the plow.

Every morning, I see Arianna shake
out the pink and white petals
of her nightly cough. They fly
from her sheets, her gown, her
long black hair. Then Lucky,
the dwarf, shoos them
from the courtyard
with his straw broom.

Nothing's ever forgot.
The swirls of wool
on the lost sheep's back
feel the pull
of the full moon.

And the woman who hides
in the olive grove
tastes of the olive's
tender bitterness.

Whether it's true or not,
it's true. The owl is heard not
with the ear, but with the heart.

Right or wrong,
wrong or right,
I plow on.

PALM READING, 1950

Into that year, 1950, you,
Roberto Zingarello, will carry your
thirty-nine years, but, at the same
time, in heart tissue, ninety-three.

In that very year, 1950,
your little bastard son, Robertino,
no need to blush, shall be born,
October 31, 7:30 p.m.

1950, when you slide
your hand along the thigh
of Marita, elite nightclub dancer,
who shows you a postcard
from a place called California.
Don't worry about us. Love,
Blanca and baby Roberto.
You tear it up, toss
it away, a bad lottery ticket.

That year, 1950, smoking
a cigarette, rolled from scraps
of other cigarettes, you take in
a wedding across the street.
What's it to you? the tilt
of your chin wants to know.

1950, and there,
at Our Lady of Beloved Solitude,
the bride, a woman you know
too well, your own mother,
laughs, rice nestling in her
hair. Your right hand goes
down, sheltering the tiny
seeds of unborn Zingarellos.

Shine? Massimo will offer,
his look stabbing your boots,
and you let him. Not for the life
of the boots, but because
his father skipped off on him.

And high rises shall rise up
on the moon in the year 2050,
you carve into wet cement, before
a store selling purple clothing.

That year, 1950, when you
throw back the thick canvas
of a delivery truck to find a large
wooden barrel of nails. The joy,
at last, of discovering one thing
not even you, Zingarello, can steal
from the future.

END OF DAYS

We sit like two padrones
in the padrone's lawnchairs,
Mario and I,
gardener and wanderer,
the brown bottle
between us. We wait
for the sunset.

The bleached mop hangs
from its nail
by the back door.
The brick wall catches
the forked shadow
of the broken
pecan limb.

The shadow, now
a lizard, now
the veins
in the back
of a man's hand.

Let them blow up the world,
my friend says.
Some fool was bound to
eventually.

The mop on the wall
does not agree
or disagree.

Let them blow up the world,
a voice crows.

The wild clover
never looked so
wild, so red.

DESIRE

Homage to Cesare Pavese

Somewhere, between my eyes, the window, the
poplars, I hug a child, a boy, no name, no face, no parents.
The poplars sway, back from the darker sky, embracing
what they resist most. I hug the boy. Stop crying, I say, stop
breathing, stop telling me I'm your father. In the room, a
body, clear jelly, pawed-out face, even that salt water root
at the center, gnawed at.

I used to sit, still like this, at a
window in the city. Waiting for her: long black braids,
rounded white collar, thin black belt, flip-flops, brown
skin the smell of swimming pools, convents, the red soil of
Sardinia. I look down at my back, the window, the poplars.
Now I know, when she comes (and she will come, she will
come), it will be through the eyes, burning off everything I
have used to keep her away.

On the streets named after
fish, if she ever, by accident, brushed against my flesh, all
they'd find by the curb, a dead pigeon. More and more, I
need to leave this body, leave the boy at the train station,
waiting for his parents, who died in a hotel fire on their
honeymoon. Leave the boy while he sleeps, kissing him once
on the forehead, and hide in a bomb shelter in the mountains,
where deserted carnival rides rust the color of ocher.

I stare
at a woman, her hands as she rubs oil into them. And I
want to swallow that white feather stuck to my upper lip,
swallow it so I can watch it burn at the edges, from light,
gravity, mass, density, distance, desire.

The porch light,
it desires to be darker. The porch door, it desires to be
slammed. The front of the house, it desires not to be seen.
A man turns off the light, lets the door slam, steps into tree
shadow. I see his back, I see a boy, a carpet over his head, I
see his back, all I can see, his back.

FORGIVENESS: INSCRIPTION FOUND INSIDE ZINGARELLO'S BIBLE

Forgive me,
friend,
nothing.

Forgive me,
then,
this.

I want to die
from the passion
for everything.

WHAT IS A MOUTH FOR BUT TO YAWN WHENEVER SOMEONE IS NOT SAYING YOUR NAME

Your name, Blanca, your name,
train car with a bag of snails on the seat,
boy who wets his pants at the sight of windmills,
conductor who sleeps clutching a river stone,
glass of grappa beside a plate of green beans.

Your name, Blanca, your name,
the price of hearing it, weighed
against the cost of saying your name,
ratio of flute to brick smokestack,
of walking stick to sleepwalking,
ratio of heartbeat to half-life of breath.

Your name, Blanca, your name,
steel door smelling of thunderstorm,
leather boot burning on the library roof,
blackbirds lifting from a soccer field,
clover spreading through a cat's ribcage.

ZINGARELLO DOESN'T LIVE HERE ANYMORE

In the carriage house, second story, sibling to the larger brick estate of old man Pomodoro, built on the wages of those who work in his tomato canning factory, to maintain the estate, its grounds and owners, who, out of profound gratitude, give those workers rent bills and babies, wine and pasta and heart attacks, for which they keep coming back to the factory for more.

At the window, where he stared at the estate house windows, where there stared back Madelena, sentenced to life in a wheelchair, some say, for the crime of confessing to her father, *But Papa, I'm a socialist*, hidden by the high iron bars entwined with wisteria surrounding the estate, those bars that greet the passerby with their litany, *Don't you wish you had it so good? Yes, some of us must live like this, to make up for the rest of you. Now move along. Don't dawdle. And keep off the property.*

At the writing table, into which the former tenant, and sometimes recluse, carved, with the tip of his bitter laugh, his, how bourgeois, how proletariat, crooked initials, and where, inside the woodgrain, lurk, as in the core of everything, tiny bacteria, who, for lack of the twelve commandments of the clock, sleep and breed, breed and sleep.

On the stairs, smelling, on a warm day, of the cat, who claimed, in the name of all future cats, this stairway, and all it commands, and, at the bottom of the stairs, the door, usually left half-open, a reminder to the wind and the sky, *Friends, this is not the end of the world.*

And, behind the carriage house, along the dirt road, the clump of sunflowers, where Mario, son of the soil, eases out a sigh, leans into the drag on his cigarette, and sunflowers, taller than a tall man, which Mario is not, they sweep and sway, in a language of sweeps and sways, speaking, to any who might inquire, *Zingarello? Oh, Zingarello. No, he doesn't live here anymore. He used to, and then, for a long time, he didn't. And he still doesn't. No, Zingarello doesn't live here anymore.*

NOTES

This book is not a translation, but an original work, composed in English. It began as an obsession with Italian film, history, and literature of the twentieth century. Soon, there was Roberto Antonio Zingarello at the doorway. Born in Milan, he began writing poetry after World War II. His influences, he once said, were "poverty, the Bible, and my mother."

At this point Zingarello is no mere persona, but a man I expect to run into one day at the drug store, diner, corner restaurant. He will be unshaven, wear a battered borsalino, and nod a greeting to me, smiling slyly. I hope these poems taken together create a biography of this man, a public and private history.

"A Few Things You Should Know About Roberto"
    Federico Garcia Lorca was killed by Franco's
    Falangists in 1936. Mussolini aided Franco in the
    Spanish Civil War.
"Why Does Everything Have to Be So Beautiful"
    Dino Campana, the author of *Canti Orfici*, was
    interned in 1918 at the psychiatric hospital of Castel
    Pulci, in Florence, where he remained until his death,
    in 1932.
"The Kitchen"
    The opening line, "The kitchen is the most surreal
    part of the house," is by Blas de Otero.
"Revenge"
    The Arditi were the black-shirted Italian WWI
    veterans that Mussolini used as the foundation for his
    Fascist rule. They were the model for Hitler's Brown
    Shirts.
"Thousands of Shouts Away: Vallejo in Russia"
    The Peruvian poet César Vallejo made three trips to
    Russia, the first in 1928.
"Ballad: For Pierre Magnol"
    The magnolia was named for the French botanist
    Pierre Magnol.
"Elegy on the Death of a Mad Dog"
    The title comes from the elegy by Oliver Goldsmith,
    ending: "The man recovered of the bite, / The dog it
    was that died."

About the Author

John Bradley was born in Brooklyn, New York, and grew up in Massachusetts, Nebraska, Long Island, and Minnesota. He is the author of *Terrestrial Music* (Curbstone Press), *War on Words* (BlazeVOX), *You Don't Know What You Don't Know* (CSU Poetry Center), and *Trancelumination* (Lowbrow Press). He is the editor of three anthologies: *Atomic Ghost: Poets Respond to the Nuclear Age* (Coffee House Press), *Learning to Glow: A Nuclear Reader* (University of Arizona Press), and *Eating the Pure Light: Homage to Thomas McGrath* (The Backwaters Press). Bradley is the recipient of two National Endowment for the Arts Fellowships and a Pushcart Prize for his poetry. He teaches at Northern Illinois University.

About the Artist

Erica Daborn received her MFA from the Royal College of Art, London. She has had solo exhibitions at the Santa Barbara Contemporary Arts Forum; the Oriel Gallery, Cardiff, Wales; and the Air Gallery, London. She has received fellowships from the MacDowell Colony, the Virginia Center for the Creative Arts, the Welsh Arts Council, and other organizations. Currently she lives in Santa Barbara and teaches at the University of Santa Barbara.

About the Washington Prize

Love-In-Idleness: The Poetry of Roberto Zingarello is the winner of the 1989 Word Works Washington Prize. John Bradley's manuscript was selected from more than 400 manuscripts submitted by American poets.

First Readers:
Maxine Combs, Geraldine Connolly, Patricia Garfinkel, Howard Gofreed, Patricia Gray, Laurie Greer, James McEuen, Peggy Miller, Paul Nijelski, Linda Stiles, Jodi Suleiman, Ian Walton.

Second Readers:
Catherine Harnett-Shaw, Elaine Maggarell, Sue Teigen.

Final Judges:
Karren Alenier, J. H. Beall, Michael Davis (Project Director), Barbara Goldberg, Robert Sargent.

Other Washington Prize Books

Nathalie F. Anderson, *Following Fred Astaire*, 1998
Michael Atkinson, *One Hundred Children Waiting for a Train*, 2001
Molly Bashaw, *The Whole Field Still Moving Inside It*, 2013
Carrie Bennett, *biography of water*, 2004
Peter Blair, *Last Heat*, 1999
Richard Carr, *Ace*, 2008
Jamison Crabtree, *Rel[AM]ent*, 2014
B.K. Fischer, St. Rage's Vault, 2012
Ann Rae Jonas, *A Diamond Is Hard But Not Tough*, 1997
Frannie Lindsay, *Mayweed*, 2009
Richard Lyons, *Fleur Carnivore*, 2005
Fred Marchant, *Tipping Point*, 1993, 2nd edition 2013
Ron Mohring, *Survivable World*, 2003
Brad Richard, *Motion Studies*, 2010
Jay Rogoff, *The Cutoff*, 1994
Prartho Sereno, *Call from Paris*, 2007, 2nd edition 2013
Enid Shomer, *Stalking the Florida Panther*, 1987, 2nd printing 1993
John Surowiecki, *The Hat City after Men Stopped Wearing Hats*, 2006
Miles Waggener, *Phoenix Suites*, 2002
Mike White, *How to Make a Bird with Two Hands*, 2011
Nancy White, *Sun, Moon, Salt*, 1992, 2nd edition 2010

About The Word Works

The Word Works, a nonprofit literary organization, publishes contemporary poetry and presents public programs. Since 1981, it has sponsored the Washington prize, a monetary award to and book publication for an American or Canadian poet. Other imprints include the Hilary Tham Capital Collection, International Editions, and The Tenth Gate Prize. A reading period for Word Works authors and finalists and semi-finalists from our contests is also held in May.

Monthly, The Word Works offers free literary programs in the Chevy Chase, MD, Café Muse series, and each summer, it holds free poetry programs in Washington, DC's Rock Creek Park. Annually in June, two high school students debut in the Joaquin Miller Poetry Series as winners of the Jacklyn Potter Young Poets Competition. Since 1974, Word Works programs have included: "In the Shadow of the Capitol," a symposium and archival project on the African American intellectual community in segregated Washington, DC; the Gunston Arts Center Poetry Series; the Poet Editor panel discussions at The Writer's Center; and Master Class workshops.

As a 501(c)3 organization, The Word Works has received awards from the National Endowment for the Arts, the National Endowment for the Humanities, the DC Commission on the Arts & Humanities, the Witter Bynner Foundation, Poets & Writers, The Writer's Center, Bell Atlantic, the David G. Taft Foundation, and others, including many generous private patrons.

The Word Works has established an archive of artistic and administrative materials in the Washington Writing archive housed in the George Washington University Gelman Library. It is a member of the Council of Literary Magazines and Presses and its books are distributed by Small Press Distribution.

More information at WordWorksBooks.org.

OTHER WORD WORKS BOOKS

THE HILARY THAM CAPITAL COLLECTION

Mel Belin, *Flesh That Was Chrysalis*
Doris Brody, *Judging the Distance*
Sarah Browning, *Whiskey in the Garden of Eden*
Grace Cavalieri, *Pine Crest Rest Home*
Christopher Conlon, *Gilbert and Garbo in Love* &
       Mary Falls: Requiem for Mrs. Surratt
Donna Denizé, *Broken Like Job*
W. Perry Epes, *Nothing Happened*
Bernadette Geyer, *The Scabbard of Her Throat*
Barbara G. S. Hagerty, *Twinzilla*
James Hopkins, *Eight Pale Women*
Brandon Johnson, *Love's Skin*
Marilyn McCabe, *Perpetual Motion*
Judith McCombs, *The Habit of Fire*
Miles David Moore, *The Bears of Paris* &
       Rollercoaster
Kathi Morrison-Taylor, *By the Nest*
Tera Vale Ragan, *Reading the Ground*
Maria Terrone, *The Bodies We Were Loaned*
Hilary Tham, *Bad Names for Women* &
       Counting
Barbara Ungar, *Charlotte Brontë, You Ruined My Life* &
       Immortal Medusa
Jonathan Vaile, *Blue Cowboy*
Rosemary Winslow, *Green Bodies*
Michele Wolf, *Immersion*
Joseph Zealberg, *Covalence*

THE TENTH GATE PRIZE

Lisa Sewell, *Impossible Object*

International Editions

Keyne Cheshire, *Murder at Jagged Rock*
Yoko Danno & James C. Hopkins, *The Blue Door*
Moshe Dor, Barbara Goldberg, Giora Leshem, eds.,
    The Stones Remember
Moshe Dor (Barbara Goldberg, trans.), *Scorched by the Sun*
Lee Sang (Myong-Hee Kim, trans.), *Crow's Eye View:*
    The Infamy of Lee Sang, Korean Poet
Vladimir Levchev (Henry Taylor, trans.), *Black Book of the*
    Endangered Species

Additional Word Works Titles

Karren L. Alenier, *Wandering on the Outside*
Karren L. Alenier, Hilary Tham, Miles David Moore, eds.,
    Winners: A Retrospective of the Washington Prize
P.T. Pfefferle, *My Coolest Shirt*
Christopher Bursk, ed., *Cool Fire*
Barbara Goldberg, *Berta Broadfoot and Pepin the Short*
Jacklyn Potter, Dwaine Rieves, Gary Stein, eds.,
    Cabin Fever: Poets at Joaquin Miller's Cabin
Robert Sargent, *Aspects of a Southern Story &*
    A Woman from Memphis

www.ingramcontent.com/pod-product-compliance
Lightning Source LLC
Chambersburg PA
CBHW030853090426
42737CB00009B/1209